ADAM HAMILTON

WHEN CHRISTIANS GET IT WRONG

Leader Guide

D1525087

Abingdon Press

Nashville

WHEN CHRISTIANS GET IT WRONG
LEADER GUIDE

ISBN 978-1-5018-0012-2

10 11 12 13 14 15 16 17 18 19 — 10 9 8 7 6 5 4 3 2 1

MANUFACTURED IN THE UNITED STATES OF AMERICA

CONTENTS

HOW TO USE THIS
LEADER GUIDE

There is a growing frustration and sometimes open hostility toward Christianity on the part of an increasing number of people today, particularly young adults. In fact, according to the research of the Barna Institute, 40% of young adults have turned away from Christianity and want nothing to do with Christians. In their 2007 book *unChristian*, David Kinnaman and Gabe Lyons outlined the Barna Institute's research with hundreds of young adults who were outside the Christian faith. They found that these young adults perceived Christians to be hypocritical, unloving, too political, anti-intellectual, insensitive, judgmental, and "anti-homosexual." My conversations with young adults substantiate their findings. Generally I have found that young people have rejected Christianity not necessarily because of beliefs, although sometimes this was the case, but more often because of the attitudes and actions of Christians they have known or observed.

When Christians Get It Wrong was born out of a conversation I had with a young man named John who had some pretty strong negative perceptions of the Christian faith. This video-based study is intended to help us listen to young adults who, like John, have been turned off, frustrated, or even hurt by Christians and to consider what Christianity might look like when we Christians get it right. The goal is to learn something from these young adults so that we may strive to be the kind of Christians who draw people to Christ rather than push them away. To do this, we will explore some of the specific criticisms young adults have of Christianity and Christians, with a specific focus on how we can be more like Jesus as we relate and communicate to those who are outside the Christian faith. Then, in the final session, we will consider how returning to the basic or core teachings of Jesus can make us more effective in helping to bring about spiritual transformation in people's lives. There is also a brief bonus video of John, the young man who inspired this study series, which groups may choose to watch at the close of the final session.

This six-week study may be used by Sunday school classes as well as a variety of other small groups meeting at various times during the week. You will want to make group members aware of the accompanying participant book, which expounds on the weekly video presentations. Participants are strongly encouraged to read the corresponding chapter in the participant book before the weekly group session. Although the book is not a required resource, it will greatly enhance the study experience and serve as a helpful resource to have on hand. Ideally, participants should have the opportunity to purchase copies of the book prior to your first group session.

A QUICK OVERVIEW

As group leader, your role will be to facilitate the weekly sessions using this leader guide and the accompanying DVD. Because no two groups are alike, this guide has been designed to give you flexibility and choice in tailoring the sessions for your group. You may choose one of the following format options, or adapt these as you wish to meet the schedule and needs of your particular group. (Note: The times indicated within parentheses are merely estimates. You may move at a faster or slower pace, making adjustments as necessary to fit your schedule.)

Basic Option: 60 minutes

Welcome / Important Reminders ....(3–5 minutes)
Opening Prayer...(2 minutes)
Biblical Foundation.......................................(3 minutes)
Video Presentation ....(15 minutes)
Group Discussion ....(30 minutes)
Closing Prayer...(< 5 minutes)

Extended Option: 90 minutes

Welcome / Important Reminders..................... (3–5 minutes)
Opening Prayer...(2 minutes)
Biblical Foundation....................................... (3 minutes)
Opening Activity.................................. (10–15 minutes)
Video Presentation..................................... (15 minutes)
Group Discussion ....(30 minutes)
Group Activity...(15 minutes)
Closing Prayer...(< 5 minutes)

You are encouraged to make Scripture and prayer regular components of the weekly group sessions. The Scripture verses provided for each session are intended to serve as a biblical foundation for the group session. Similarly, the opening and closing prayers are intended to "cover" the group session in prayer, acknowledging that we desperately need God's help if we are to receive and address criticism with grace and understanding and make the changes necessary to be more loving and welcoming to those who are unimpressed with and sometimes even hostile toward Christianity. Feel free to use the printed prayers or create your own.

IMPORTANT REMINDERS

Be sure to take time at the beginning of each session, before the opening prayer, to review the following reminders with the group:

- The purpose of this study is not to debate beliefs or opinions but to help you hear and understand the perceptions and feelings of young adults outside the Christian faith.
- Some issues and beliefs are complex and multifaceted and, therefore, will result in multifaceted perspectives; yet as followers of Christ we are called to demonstrate respect, acceptance, and love toward those with whom we disagree.
- This session is not intended to be a debate or a gripe session but an opportunity to grow as disciples of Jesus Christ as we learn more about the perceptions of young adults and how we can be more like Christ in communicating and interacting with those who are outside the Christian faith.
- Be willing to let go of your biases and to question your assumptions. You will agree with some points and disagree with others. But as you are willing to see things from the perspective of young adults outside the Christian faith, you will come to discover how you may be a more influential representative of Christ in a skeptical world.

Another effective way to avoid getting off track and to prepare participants for constructive, grace-filled dialogue is to have someone read aloud one or both of the following Scriptures prior to group discussion:

Always be humble, gentle, and patient, accepting each other in love. You are joined together with peace through the Spirit, so make every effort to continue together in this way. (*Ephesians 4:2-3, NCV*)

Stay away from foolish and stupid arguments, because you know they grow into quarrels. And a servant of the Lord must not quarrel but must be kind to everyone, a good teacher, and patient. The Lord's servant must gently teach those who disagree. Then maybe God will let them change their minds so they can accept the truth. (2 Timothy 2:23-25, NCV)

LEADER HELPS

In addition to the components outlined in the suggested format options, the following "leader helps" are provided to equip you for each group session:

Main Idea (session theme)

Session Goals (objectives for the group session)

Key Insights (summary of main points from the video)

Leader Extra (additional information related to topic)

Notable Quote (noteworthy quote from the participant book)

(A couple of sessions also include suggestions for further study or reflection.) You may use these helps for your personal preparation only, or you may choose to incorporate them into the group session in some way. For example, you might choose to write the main idea and/or session goals on a board or chart prior to the beginning of class, review the key insights from the video either before or after group discussion, incorporate the leader extra into group discussion, or close with the notable quote.

HELPFUL HINTS

Here are a few helpful hints for preparing and leading the weekly group sessions:

- Become familiar with the material before the group session. If possible, watch the DVD segment in advance.
- Choose the various components you will use during the group session, including the specific discussion questions you plan to cover. (Highlight these or put a checkmark beside them.) Remember, you do not have to use all of the questions provided, and you even can create your own.
- Secure a TV and DVD player in advance; oversee room setup.
- Begin and end on time.
- Be enthusiastic. Remember, you set the tone for the class.
- Create a climate of participation, encouraging individuals to participate as they feel comfortable.
- Communicate the importance of group discussions and group exercises.
- To stimulate group discussion, consider reviewing the key insights first and then asking participants to tell what they saw as the highlights of the video.
- If no one answers at first, don't be afraid of a little silence. Count to seven silently; then say something such as, "Would anyone like to go first?" If no one responds, venture an answer yourself. Then ask for comments and other responses.
- Model openness as you share with the group. Group members will follow your example. If you share at a surface level, everyone else will follow suit.
- Draw out participants without asking them to share what they are unwilling to share. Make eye contact with someone and say something such as, "How about someone else?"
- Encourage multiple answers or responses before moving on.

- Ask "Why?" or "Why do you believe that?" to help continue a discussion and give it greater depth.
- Affirm others' responses with comments such as, "Great" or "Thanks" or "Good insight"—especially if this is the first time someone has spoken during the group session.
- Give everyone a chance to talk, but keep the conversation moving. Moderate to prevent a few individuals from doing all of the talking.
- Monitor your own contributions. If you are doing most of the talking, back off so that you do not train the group to not respond.
- Remember that you do not have to have all the answers. Your job is to keep the discussion going and encourage participation.
- Honor the time schedule. If a session is running longer than expected, get consensus from the group before continuing beyond the agreed upon ending time.
- Consider involving group members in various aspects of the group session, such as asking for volunteers to run the DVD, read the prayers or say their own, read the Scripture, and so forth.

Above all, remember to pray. Pray for God to prepare and guide you; pray for your group members by name and for what God may do in their lives; pray for participants to be sensitive, respectful, and loving in all they say; and pray for God's presence and leading before each group session. Prayer will both encourage and empower you for the weeks ahead.

Now, let's get started!

WEEK 1

WHEN CHRISTIANS
ARE UNCHRISTIAN

Main Idea: The critique of non-Christians that they perceive us to be judgmental, hypocritical, and unloving should serve as a warning that many of us have become the very Pharisees Jesus preached against. We get it right when we love rather than condemn those who are outside the church.

GETTING STARTED

Session Goals

This session is intended to help participants . . .

- recognize the disparity between the love Christians are meant to display and what young adults often witness or experience
- identify four things Jesus warned his followers against related to hypocrisy
- understand that we are all recovering Pharisees
- recognize that we get it right when we love and give, work for justice, demonstrate kindness, and befriend rather than condemn those who are outside the church

Welcome / Important Reminders

Welcome participants and review the important reminders on p. 8.

Opening Prayer

Dear Lord, we acknowledge that we all act in ways that are unchristian at times. Each of us struggles with the tendency to have wrong motives, be critical and judgmental of others, miss the point, and be insensitive and mean-spirited. It is so easy to point out the sins of others while ignoring our own, major in the minors while failing to do the really important things you demand of us, and pretend to be something we're not. When we act in these ways, we are not following the example of love that you modeled for us and taught us to follow. We're all recovering Pharisees, Lord, and we know that only by recognizing our tendency to be Pharisees do we have the hope of remaining in recovery. Teach us to be more like you, Lord. Fill us with your Spirit so that that others will see fruit in our lives—love, joy, peace, patience, kindness, generosity, faithfulness, gentleness, and self-control—and be drawn to our faith. Amen.

Biblical Foundation

Now all the tax collectors and sinners were coming near to listen to him. And the Pharisees and the scribes were grumbling and saying, "This fellow welcomes sinners and eats with them." (Luke 15:1-2)

Opening Activity

Read aloud the following excerpt from the participant book:

Young people are more secular than ever before. . . . About one in five . . . are either atheist or agnostic or [have] no faith. That compares to about one in every twenty people . . . over the age of 60. Essentially, people believe Christianity is no longer like Jesus intended. That's why they say it is unchristian. They believe essentially that we're hypocritical . . . judgmental . . . sheltered . . . too political . . . anti-homosexual . . . too focused on getting converts—that we're proselytizers. This negative set of perceptions over-whelms any favorable ideas about seeing us doing good deeds [in] the world. They see this overwhelmingly negative picture of the church, and they reject Jesus and the church because they don't want to be associated with that kind of people.   —David Kinnaman

Discuss: *Why do you think young adults today have such an over-whelmingly negative picture of Christianity and Christians?*

LEARNING TOGETHER

Video Presentation

Play the DVD segment for Week 1, *When Christians Are Unchristian.*

Running Time: 15:47

Key Insights

1. Most non-Christians know that Jesus stood for love, which is why it feels particularly off-putting to them when those who claim to follow Jesus act in unloving ways.
2. Jesus taught that God's primary rule was love and that God's interest wasn't in condemning those who were "sinners" but in drawing them to himself.
3. Jesus warned his followers about four things related to hypocrisy: wrong motives, judging others, majoring in the minors, and being two-faced.
4. We need to ask ourselves four questions:
   - Am I using God, or am I allowing God to use me?
   - Do I point out other people's sins without recognizing my own?

- Have I forgotten Jesus' assurance that our love for one another is how the world will know we are his followers?
- Have I cleaned the outside of the cup but neglected the inside?

5. We're all guilty of hypocrisy, and it's only in recognizing and admitting this that we have any hope of becoming more like Christ.

6. Jesus commands us not to judge, warns us against hypocrisy, and calls us to love all—both our neighbors and those with whom we do not see eye to eye.

7. When we get it right, others see the fruit of the Spirit in our lives—love, joy, peace, patience, kindness, generosity, faithfulness, gentleness, and self-control (Galatians 5:22-23)—and are drawn to our faith.

Leader Extra
Reducing Spirituality to Moral Benchmarks

What is behind many—not all, but many—charges and accusations against the character and integrity of Christians is the demand for perfection in the life of anyone who claims to be a Christian and urges others to consider Christianity as well. This is not, of course, the true meaning of a hypocrite, but even more to the point, it is not an accurate understanding of what it means to enter into the Christian life. Yet the world holds us to it, because we hold ourselves—and others—to it. We fall prey to the charge of hypocrisy because we have reduced spirituality to a list of moral benchmarks coupled with a good dose of judgmentalism. The only way to regain our footing is to remind ourselves—and others—that an authentic Christian is simply someone who has made the decision to believe in Jesus as his forgiver and then attempt to follow him as his leader. But *nowhere* in this series of events is perfection *or* sinlessness. Rather, there is simply the intentional effort and sincere desire to recognize God as, well, God. . . . Simply put, we must stop presenting ourselves as the message and begin presenting Jesus as the message. There will be disappointment with Christians as long as there are imperfect people. Since all Christians are imperfect, there will always be disappointment. So we must stop having the message of Christ tied to our butchered efforts.

—author Jim White, quoted in *unChristian*
(Baker Books, 2007); pp. 65–66

Group Discussion

Note: More questions are provided than you may have time for. Select those you would like your group to discuss.

1. Read Matthew 22:36-39; Matthew 5:43-48; and John 13:34-35. What did Jesus teach us about love in these verses? Why do you think there is often such a disparity between the love we are meant to display and what young adults often witness or experience?

2. How did Jesus treat "sinners"? Who were the only ones Jesus had words of judgment for in the Gospels? What angered him the most about these people and why?

3. Read Matthew 6:2. What warning does Jesus give regarding giving, praying, and fasting? How can the desire for attention, praise, or a good image spoil our service to God? What are some ways we can guard against wrong motives?

4. Read Matthew 7:4-5. Why do you think we are so prone to point out the sins of others without recognizing our own? How does this demonstrate a kind of superiority and spiritual or moral pride? Why is pride even more dangerous to the soul than the sins we might be denouncing in others?

5. Read Matthew 23:23-24. What was Jesus rebuking the Pharisees for in these verses? What are some ways we "forget to love" today—both as individuals and as the church? How can we help one another to cultivate spiritual honesty?

6. Read Matthew 23:25. How can we know if our religion is merely "window dressing"? Why do you think that focusing on the superficialities prevents heart change and

transformation? What can help us to live out what we say we believe so that God's work is accomplished in our world?

7. If no one is perfect and all human beings are Pharisees to one degree or another, what is the real issue behind the criticism that Christians are hypocritical and unloving? Why is it so important for us to recognize our tendency to be hypocritical? How might this change the way we communicate and interact with those outside the Christian faith?

8. Read Galatians 5:22-23. How did the apostle Paul describe what it looks like when followers of Christ "get it right"? How would you describe in your own words what it looks like to follow Jesus' example of love?

9. How has this discussion helped or challenged you?

Group Activity

Read aloud Leader Extra: "Reducing Spirituality to Moral Benchmarks."

Discuss: *In light of Jim White's comments, what can we do to change the perception among young adults that Christians are hypocritical? Practically speaking, what are some ways we can stop presenting ourselves as the message and, instead, present Jesus Christ as the message?* Write ideas on a board or chart.

WRAPPING UP

Notable Quote

My experience with non-religious people is that they are not expecting Christians to be perfect. In fact, one young adult said, "I don't mind that you Christians don't live up to your ideals. I don't live up to all of my ideals either. In the end, I guess we're all hypocrites, it's just that . . . it seems that many Christians haven't figured this out yet." What makes the hypocrisy of Christians the more onerous is when we go about pointing out the sins of others.

—Adam Hamilton

Closing Prayer

Dear God, we want to be filled with your love and goodness all the time. But we're not there yet, so sometimes we're tempted to fake it—and that can get ugly. Help us to live authentically in your love and grace, letting go of our need to look good even when we aren't. Teach us to own our struggles and claim your power to transform us. Amen.

WEEK 2

CHRISTIANS, SCIENCE, AND POLITICS

Main Idea: If we want to get it right in science and politics, we need to be open-minded, humble, and teachable, recognizing that we do not have all the truth.

GETTING STARTED

Session Goals

This session is intended to help participants . . .

- recognize that many young adults are alienated by the belief that much of what we know from modern science is incompatible with Christian teaching
- consider the role that fear plays in shaping how some Christians approach science
- briefly explore two major points of debate: creation and evolution
- see science as an important companion in the quest for knowledge and truth and a catalyst for their worship of a magnificent God
- consider why it is a dangerous thing when the church or individual Christians become "married" to either political party
- engage in the political arena in a way that is consistent with their faith
- be open-minded and teachable, recognizing they do not have all the truth

Welcome / Important Reminders

Welcome participants and review the important reminders on p. 8.

Opening Prayer

Dear God, many young people today have the perception that we Christians are anti-intellectual—that we check our brains at the door when we enter church—and that we are biased and judgmental in our political views. This is hurtful to hear, and our tendency is to become defensive. Help us not to react to these criticisms, Lord, but to hear and understand why young people outside the church see us this way. Help us to be objective rather than subjective, open-minded rather than closed-minded, and humble rather than proud. Remind us today that we model a Christ-like attitude when we show patience and understanding and love. Help us to be teachable, Lord, recognizing that we do not have all the truth. Amen.

Biblical Foundation

In the beginning when God created the heavens and the earth, the earth was a formless void and darkness covered the face of the deep, while a wind from God swept over the face of the waters. Then God said, "Let there be light"; and there was light. And God saw that the light was good; and God separated the light from the darkness. God called the light Day, and the darkness he called Night. And there was evening and there was morning, the first day. And God said, "Let there be a dome in the midst of the waters, and let it separate the waters from the waters." So God made the dome and separated the waters that were under the dome from the waters that were above the dome. And it was so. God called the dome Sky. And there was evening and there was morning, the second day. (Genesis 1:1-8)

"Teacher, we know that you are sincere, and teach the way of God in accordance with truth, and show deference

22

to no one; for you do not regard people with partiality. Tell us, then, what you think. Is it lawful to pay taxes to the emperor, or not?" . . . He said to them, "Give . . . to the emperor the things that are the emperor's, and to God the things that are God's." When they heard this, they were amazed; and they left him and went away. (Matthew 22:16b-17, 21b-22)

Opening Activity
Write the following statement on a board or chart:

> *The more you grow in your faith and the more profoundly you know God, the more you know that you do not know.*

Ask participants if they agree with this statement. Then invite them to share ways they have come to this realization personally.

Discuss: *How have you come to know that there is much you do not know? Why is it important to be open-minded and teachable?*

LEARNING TOGETHER

Video Presentation
Play the DVD segment for Week 2, *Christians, Science, and Politics.*
Running Time: 16:07

Key Insights
1. On June 22, 1633, a tribunal of the Roman Catholic Church pronounced Galileo a heretic for promoting a scientific idea that contradicted the church's teaching. Galileo's trial was the start of an accelerating process in which scientific discoveries have drawn the wrath of Christians who complain that the new ideas undermine their faith.

2. Many bright, thinking people find themselves increasingly alienated by the belief of some Christians that much of what we know from modern science is incompatible with Christian teaching.

3. Fear plays a major role in shaping how some Christians approach science. They fear science because they think that it either competes with faith or is actively engaged in destroying faith by disproving or debunking what they believe.

4. One of the major points of debate has been the Genesis account of Creation. Some Christians have insisted that science must conform itself to a literal reading of the verses in Genesis. However, the Genesis account is not meant to teach us *how* God created but *that* God created.

5. Scripture and faith, not science, teach us about the meaning of life and human existence. Science teaches us about the way creation works. Scripture and faith teach the *Who* and *why*; science teaches the *how* and *when*.

6. In the past century, many Christians were vocal in their opposition to evolution. The most famous battle between Christianity and evolution was played out in a courtroom in Dayton, Tennessee, in July 1925. William Jennings Bryan won the case, but Christianity appeared the loser. In the latter part of the twentieth century, the battle was on again as fundamentalists challenged textbooks and demanded that creationism be taught alongside evolution.

7. Evolution is only a description of a process that seems to explain how simpler organisms may evolve into more complex life forms over time. It is not incompatible with Christianity until the theory is misused and applied to ethics, or until someone uses it to suggest that there is no purpose or order to creation. Millions of Christians believe that the two are not incompatible.

8. Science magnifies God by helping us to see the exquisite and marvelous workings of creation, giving us a greater sense of awe at the Creator.

9. We get it wrong as Christians when we see science as a threat to our faith or try to make the Bible a scientific

textbook. We get it right when we see science as an important companion in the quest for knowledge and truth and a catalyst for our worship of a magnificent God.

10. Neither the Republican Party nor the Democratic Party has a corner on the truth, and it is a dangerous thing when the church or individual Christians become "married" to either political party.

11. Some Christians, in the name of God, say and do things in the realm of politics that are the antithesis of the gospel.

12. The apostle Paul offers instructive words in Ephesians 4:29-32 for how we Christians are meant to conduct ourselves in all areas of life, including politics:
    • Avoid unwholesome talk and speak only what benefits those who listen.
    • Get rid of bitterness, rage, anger, slander, and malice.
    • Be kind, compassionate, and forgiving.

13. Jesus gave us an important word about politics when he told us to give to the emperor the things that belong to the emperor and to God the things that belong to God. Just as Caesar's image is on the coin, so God's image is on our souls. We must not allow a party, or a leader, or even our nation to become for us an idol. We must give our allegiance—our souls and our hearts—to God alone.

14. We get it right in politics when we work for justice with grace, truth, and love; fight for what we believe in a way that is consistent with our faith; and give our allegiance to God.

15. The more we grow in our faith, the more we know that there is much we do not know. A humble, teachable spirit and an open mind help us to model a Christ-like attitude.

Leader Extra

Four Approaches to the Genesis Account of Creation

1. Young-earth Biblical Literalist View (creation science)
• Genesis 1 accurately represents the basic facts surrounding creation; Creation took place in six twenty-four-hour days.

- Universal flood covered the planet with water.
- Sum of years calculated using the genealogies of the Old Testament is considered the actual age of the planet; our planet is less than 10,000 years old.
- Dinosaurs and humans walked the planet at the same time, but dinosaurs, like many animals, are not mentioned in the Genesis story.
- Flood is likely explanation for demise of dinosaurs; pressure created by weight of flood waters created fossils.
- Was the dominant approach to the Creation account for nearly three thousand years.

2. Old-earth Biblical Literalist View

- Takes the Creation story literally yet allows for some "wiggle room."
- Each day described in Genesis 1 could be a period or an epoch spanning millions and millions of years ("With the Lord one day is like a thousand years, and a thousand years are like one day." —2 Peter 3:8).
- Accepts the dating of scientists who say the earth could be as old as 4.6 billion years.
- Gap theory: Genesis 1:1-3 indicates the possibility of a vast period of time during which cataclysmic events might have taken place.

    Verse 1: After God creates the heavens and the earth, there is a gap for God's creative work with dinosaurs and all kinds of creatures.

    Verse 2: The earth is covered in darkness and water, perhaps the result of an asteroid hitting the earth—which is a proposed reason for the demise of the dinosaurs.

    Verse 3: Re-creation of the planet.

3. Naturalistic and Mythological View

- The Genesis story has little credibility for the modern era; it is a myth for prescientific people who needed the concept of God to explain what they could not understand.

- Evolutionary theory alone is sufficient to explain all that exists.
- Essentially dismisses the Genesis account; unacceptable to most Christians.

4. Biblical-scientific Synthesis View
- Genesis account was not meant to teach the *how* and *when* of creation, only the *Who* and *why*.
- Genesis account does not stand counter to scientific discoveries but serves a higher purpose; it is to be read and taken seriously as a statement of faith in God.
- God has inspired the words, but God's words are meant to assure all people that God is the Creator. With this assurance, we can freely engage in scientific research and remain open to new discoveries.
- Proponents are not threatened by science exploring the *how* of creation. They only serve to heighten the sense of awe at God.

Leader Extra
Misuses of the Theory of Evolution

1) Evolution is an explanation of life without the need for God.
2) Life was simply the result of chance. There is no meaning, purpose, order, or plan to life; all is chance. Survival and reproduction are the ultimate goals of life.
3) Evolution is a means of reinforcing racist ideas; the most evolved human beings are those who look most like a particular race or group (e.g., Hitler's philosophy).
4) Evolution is a liberating theory giving freedom from outmoded concepts of divine law; it gives individuals permission to pursue their own lifestyles without guilt; no ultimate right or wrong.

Group Discussion

Note: More questions are provided than you may have time for. Select those you would like your group to discuss.

1. What was the scientific idea that prompted a tribunal of the Roman Catholic Church to pronounce Galileo a heretic? Why did they believe Galileo's ideas were heretical?

2. How have some Christians continued to push back at scientific advances through the centuries? Why do some Christians think that much of what we know from modern science is incompatible with Christian teaching? Do you agree or disagree, and why?

3. What are some of the concerns that can motivate a Christian to have a suspicious or fearful attitude toward science? Do you believe such fears are legitimate or unfounded, and why?

4. Some Christians treat the Bible as a science textbook, insisting that any scientific theory that does not conform to it is in error. Why is this problematic for many young adults?

5. Read aloud the first account of Creation found in Genesis 1:1–2:3. Note the order of events and the assumptions about the structure of the world. In a world where many people worshipped the sun, moon, stars, and the forces of nature as the ultimate realities, what revolutionary religious claim does this passage put forth? What is the story's central focus: the details of "how" Earth was created or God as the creative agent behind it all?

6. This first Creation story makes some sweeping assertions, such as that humans are created in the image of God and that God made certain portions of time holy. Can statements such as these be proved or disproved scientifically (i.e. tested by observation)? What spiritual truth(s) do they convey?

7. Now read aloud the second Creation account found in Genesis 2:4-25. How is this account different from and similar to the first? What important ideas does this Creation

story include that were absent from the first one? What significant ideas from the first one does this one omit? If God had put you in charge of collecting the materials for the Bible, would you have included both of these stories? Explain your reasons.

8. How would you characterize the debate about evolution that has taken place in the past century? Why do some Christians reject the theory of evolution? Why do other Christians believe the theory of evolution is not incompatible with Christianity?

9. Can the theory of evolution ever be misused, and if so, how? See Leader Extra: "Misuses of the Theory of Evolution."

10. How does science help to magnify God and serve as a catalyst for worship? Share a time when science opened your eyes in some way to the magnitude and glory of God, filling you with awe.

11. How would you summarize what it looks like when Christians "get it right" in the area of science?

12. What does it mean to say that individual Christians or the church are "married" to a political party? Why is this dangerous?

13. Without discussing specifics, cite some of the ways that Christians, in the name of God, say and do things in the realm of politics that are the antithesis of the gospel. Read aloud Ephesians 4:29-32. How can these words of the apostle Paul help us to conduct ourselves appropriately, not only in politics but also in every area of life?

14. Read aloud Matthew 22:17-21. What important insight was Jesus making in these verses?

15. How would you summarize what it looks like when Christians "get it right" in the area of politics?

16. What happens when Christians have an open-minded and teachable attitude in the areas of science and politics? What effect does this have on young adults who are outside the church?

17. How has this discussion helped or challenged you?

Group Activity

Have someone read aloud Ephesians 4:29-32. Discuss the following: *How can the principles in these verses change our conversations with one another, or with others outside this group, about issues of science and faith? About issues of politics and faith? Which phrase in this passage speaks most directly to your faith journey and why?*

WRAPPING UP

Notable Quote

One thing that can help us to get it right in both science and politics is to be open-minded. When we are closed-minded, refusing to listen to others' ideas or treating those who hold opposing viewpoints with contempt, we are not modeling a Christ-like attitude. But we show the patience, understanding, and love of Christ when we are teachable and show respect to others—when we act with kindness and are "quick to listen, slow to speak, slow to anger" (James 1:19). We are teachable when, with humility, we recognize that we do not have all the truth.   —Adam Hamilton

Closing Prayer

Lord God, you created us with minds that ask questions and have the analytical ability to pursue answers. You also gave us the capacity to gaze in wonder at the beauty of creation, be inwardly stirred by music or painting or dance, and to gasp in awe at the touch of a baby's tiny fingers. Teach us how science and faith can be allies in helping us live our lives effectively for you. Amen.

WEEK 3

WHEN SPEAKING OF OTHER RELIGIONS

Main Idea: The most powerful form of Christian witness is expressing authentic love, compassion, mercy, and kindness toward others.

GETTING STARTED

Session Goals

This session is intended to help participants . . .

- recognize how Christians often make non-Christians feel by the way they talk and act toward them
- discern the wideness of God's mercy
- explore three ways that Christians through the ages have answered the question, "How wide is God's mercy?"
- consider what kind of witness they will be

Welcome / Important Reminders

Welcome participants and review the important reminders on p. 8.

Opening Prayer

Lord Jesus, at times we have refused to listen to the thoughts and beliefs of those who do not share our beliefs. We have been arrogant and dismissive toward them, and we have caused them to feel excluded or judged—whether intentionally or unintentionally. As a result of our unloving words, attitudes, and actions, we have actually turned people away from you. Forgive us, Lord. Help us to be more like you, drawing others to you through our humility, respect, love, compassion, mercy, and kindness. As we explore our beliefs about salvation and the wideness of your mercy, may our hearts and minds be open to your Holy Spirit and our attitudes and words be full of grace. Amen.

Biblical Foundation

> *Finally, all of you, have unity of spirit, sympathy, love for one another, a tender heart, and a humble mind. Do not repay evil for evil or abuse for abuse; but, on the contrary, repay with a blessing. It is for this that you were called—that you might inherit a blessing. . . . Always be ready to make your defense to anyone who demands from you an accounting for the hope that is in you; yet do it with gentleness and reverence. (1 Peter 3:8-9, 15b-16a)*

Opening Activity

Acknowledge that we have a tendency to divide the world into "us" and "them." Ask: *As you see the world, which persons or groups of people—including faith groups—fall into the category of "them"?* List these on a board or chart under the heading "them." (If participants are reluctant to answer, be prepared to offer the first response.) Have someone read aloud Acts 11:2-18.

Discuss: *How does Peter's vision—which reversed his view of the Roman troops in his land—speak to your view of "them"?*

LEARNING TOGETHER

Video Presentation
Play the DVD segment for Week 3, *When Speaking of Other Religions.*

Running Time: 16:13

Key Insights
1. When we refuse to listen to the thoughts and beliefs of people who are not Christians, are arrogant toward them and dismissive of them, and cause them to feel excluded or judged, we turn people away from Christ.
2. The belief that only those who have personally received Jesus Christ as Lord and Savior will enter heaven leaves at least 4.2 billion of those currently alive who are going to hell. For many young adults, this is a strange picture of a God who is said to love human beings deeply.
3. Christians through the ages have answered the question of the wideness of God's mercy in three ways:
   1) Christian Universalism – all humanity ultimately will be reconciled to God
   2) Christian Exclusivism – anyone who has not personally trusted in Christ cannot enter heaven
   3) Christian Inclusivism – Jesus died for the sins of the world, but God can give the gift of salvation to anyone God chooses based upon the criteria God chooses
4. The challenge of Christian Universalism is that it removes our human freedom to reject God's invitation of salvation. Most Scriptures on the subject point to the fact that God invites but does not force.
5. In its harshest, yet most consistent form, Christian Exclusivism excludes from heaven all children who died without receiving Christ, those with mental disabilities who did not receive Christ, and any who have never heard the good news of Jesus Christ. For this reason, many Christians today

hold a more moderate Exclusivist view, believing that God will judge those who had absolutely no opportunity to receive Christ, including children and the mentally handicapped, according to how they responded to what they could know of God (the light they were given).

6. According to Christian Inclusivism, it is possible for God to give the gift of salvation to those who have sought to love and serve God even if they have never heard the gospel or have not fully understood or accepted it. For those who have faith in God and a desire for salvation but who may not fully understand where salvation comes from or the name by which salvation is given, God looks at the heart and judges according to the light of the knowledge those persons have access to.

7. Salvation is by grace. We are saved by God's initiative because of God's love, God's righteousness, God's kindness, and God's mercy. All we bring to the table is faith. We trust that there is a God who loves us, who has called us, and who offers us the gift of salvation. Ideally this faith is in Jesus Christ, if we have had the opportunity to hear and understand the gospel. But many people have not had that opportunity.

8. The apostle Peter called Christians to witness to their faith by living holy lives, showing humility, respect, and love. The most powerful form of Christian witness is expressing authentic love, compassion, mercy, and kindness toward others.

Leader Extra

Scriptures Commonly Cited in Support of Exclusivism and Inclusivism

Exclusivism

"Those who believe in him are not condemned; but those who do not believe are condemned already, because they have not believed in the name of the only Son of God." (John 3:18)

"My sheep hear my voice. I know them, and they follow me. I give them eternal life, and they will never perish. No one will snatch them out of my hand." (John 10:27-28)

Jesus said to her, "I am the resurrection and the life. Those who believe in me, even though they die, will live, and everyone who lives and believes in me will never die." (John 11:25-26)

Jesus said to him, "I am the way, and the truth, and the life. No one comes to the Father except through me." (John 14:6)

"Everyone therefore who acknowledges me before others, I also will acknowledge before my Father in heaven; but whoever denies me before others, I also will deny before my Father in heaven." (Matthew 10:32-33)

Others:
Acts 4:11-12
Romans 1:16
Romans 3:20-26
Romans 10:9
1 John 2:23
1 John 5:11-12

Inclusivism
"Whoever is not against us is for us." (Mark 9:40)

"Indeed, God did not send the Son into the world to condemn the world, but in order that the world might be saved through him." (John 3:17)

"For the bread of God is that which comes down from heaven and gives life to the world." (John 6:33)

"And I, when I am lifted up from the earth, will draw all people to myself." (John 12:32)

Others:
Acts 10:34-35
Romans 2:6-16
Romans 5:18
Colossians 1:20
1 Timothy 4:10
2 Peter 3:9
1 John 2:2

Leader Extra
Biblical Examples of Inclusivity

Genesis 11:27–12:3
Sometimes we read God's call and promise to Abraham as indicating God's desire to shut people out—to say, "I only love this person and his family." Yet the language of God's promise points to God's broader, widely inclusive purpose for the human family. God's covenant with Abraham was meant to bless not a select group but "all peoples." God chose Abraham, not because he was better than everyone else, but because he responded to God—even in Ur and Haran (modern Iraq).

2 Kings 5:1-14
A general from Syria had leprosy. A captured Israelite girl said she knew about a prophet who could heal him. The king in Samaria thought it an enemy's ruse; the Syrian was at first too proud to accept the prophet's help. Yet across all the religious and national fears, God worked for healing and understanding. The unnamed Israelite girl is one of the Bible's unsung heroes. Taken in a raid and dragged from her home, she still wished good for Naaman and pointed him to the source of help.

Matthew 2:1-11

In this story, we meet King Herod, Israel's leading priests and teachers of the law, and the wise men from the East. Note that not only members of the "correct" religious group were told about Jesus' birth but also eastern wise men. God's people might have been exclusive, but God wasn't! Note also that it was the wise men who knew the most "correct" religious answers. Finally, both the wise men and King Herod expressed a desire to worship the new-born king, but only the wise men were serious about that. This story gives us some insight into God's attitude toward "insiders" and "outsiders."

John 4:4-24

In Jesus' day, Jewish rabbis rarely had contact with Samaritan women, as this woman's shock shows. Notice verse 19 and following, where she tries to avoid a personal exchange by raising a theological dispute. Jesus refuses the bait. What matters, he says, is worshipping God in spirit and truth. It's clear that for many Samaritans and Jews, "truth" meant having a correct intellectual belief about the right place to worship. But Jesus was using the word to describe more than correct ideas and language. He was referring not only to our intellect but also to our heart. Despite the risks of misunderstanding or damage to his reputation, Jesus chose to have this conversation with the Samaritan woman in order to offer her the living water she needed.

Leader Extra

Christian Inclusivism, Karl Rahner, and the Anonymous Christian

Within Christian Inclusivism is the idea of the "anonymous Christian," a concept introduced by Jesuit theologian Karl Rahner that says people who are not Christians can still be saved through Christ. Rahner suggested that faithful practitioners of other religions are essentially "anonymous Christians" because they have responded to the divine beckoning in their cultural and religious context by surrendering and living a devout life. They have accepted the saving grace of God, through Christ, even though they may never have heard the gospel. In other words, anonymous Christians have never had a true encounter with Christianity, but they have responded positively to the revelation of God that they have been given. As a result, they are in a state of grace, though they do not know it.

Objections to the concept of the anonymous Christian include that it is arrogant, because it assigns to people of other faiths a name they would never give themselves, and that it is not truly inclusive, because it assumes that Christianity is the one universal truth. Critics say that essentially Christians are claiming salvation for followers of other religions by placing them under the Christian umbrella, so to speak, even if only "anonymously." Another objection is that it eliminates the pressing need for Christian evangelism, because one can be saved without becoming a professing Christian.

Group Discussion

Note: More questions are provided than you may have time for. Select those you would like your group to discuss.

1. Think of a time when you felt excluded, dismissed, or judged by a person or group. How interested would you have been afterward to genuinely listen to this individual or group? Why? How do our words and actions toward those who are not Christians similarly impact our effectiveness as witnesses for Jesus Christ?

2. Do you, like many young adults, ever struggle to reconcile a loving God with the idea that those who have not personally received Jesus Christ as Lord and Savior will not enter heaven? Why or why not?

3. Briefly discuss Christian Universalism—the belief that all humanity ultimately will be reconciled to God. What do you find appealing or convincing about this belief, and why? What do you find challenging or difficult to accept, and why?

4. Briefly discuss Christian Exclusivism—the belief that anyone who has not personally trusted in Christ cannot enter heaven. What do you find appealing or convincing about this belief, and why? What do you find challenging or difficult to accept, and why?

5. What exception do moderate Exclusivists make? What do you find appealing or convincing about moderate Exclusivism, and why? What do you find challenging or difficult to accept, and why?

6. Briefly discuss Christian Inclusivism—the belief that Jesus died for the sins of the world, but that God can give the gift of salvation to anyone God chooses based on the criteria God chooses. What do you find appealing or convincing about this belief, and why? What you do find challenging or difficult to accept, and why?

7. Compare and contrast moderate Exclusivism and Christian Inclusivism. On what do they agree? How are they different? How is the exception taken by moderate Exclusivists expanded by Christian Inclusivists? If you believe that God's mercy is wide enough for those who had no opportunity to receive Christ, do you also believe God's mercy is wide enough for those who did not fully understand or accept the gospel? Why or why not?

8. Some Christians say that Exclusivism is too narrow—that it limits or restricts God's grace. Would you agree or disagree, and why?

9. Other Christians say that Inclusivism ignores the importance of choosing and professing Christ or receiving God's gift of grace. Would you agree or disagree, and why?

10. Briefly review and discuss scriptural support for both Christian Exclusivism and Christian Inclusivism. Refer to Leader Extra: "Scriptures Commonly Cited in Support of Exclusivism and Inclusivism" (see also pp. 48–50 in the participant book). What other Scriptures or biblical stories come to mind for either view? (See also Leader Extra:

"Biblical Examples of Inclusivity.") Note: Remind participants that this is not intended to be a debate but an exploration of ideas and perspectives.

11. Read aloud Ephesians 2:4-9. According to the apostle Paul, how does salvation work? What is required of us—what do we bring to the table? How do you think this applies to those who have not had the opportunity to hear and understand the gospel?

12. Discuss Karl Rahner's concept of the anonymous Christian and the objections raised by critics (see Leader Extra: "Christian Inclusivism, Karl Rahner, and the Anonymous Christian"). What do you think someone of another faith might think about the concept of being an "anonymous Christian"?

13. What are your thoughts about the objection that Inclusivism eliminates the pressing need for evangelism? Do you believe that evangelism—sharing the good news of Jesus Christ—is primarily about salvation, or are there other reasons for telling others about Christ?

14. Read aloud 1 Peter 3:8-9, 15. How does the apostle Peter call Christians to witness to their faith? How can this be a powerful Christian witness to those outside the faith?

15. When it comes to being an effective Christian witness, why is it important to be willing to find common ground and take risks? Share from personal experience, as you are willing.

16. How has this discussion helped or challenged you?

Group Activity

Read aloud Acts 17:16-34. Say: *In Athens, the "other religions" capital of his world, the apostle Paul gave us a model for dealing respectfully and lovingly with people of different faith traditions while still declaring his own faith clearly. In verse 28, he even quotes a Cretan philosopher named Epimenides and the Stoic poet Aratus.*

Discuss:

- *The apostle Paul knew how strongly God feels about idol worship and was familiar with Psalm 96:5, which says that "all the gods of the peoples are idols." A common stereotype of Paul (and all Christians after him) would picture him denouncing the Athenians as pagans, idolaters, and libertines destined for hell. How would you compare Paul's actual speech with that stereotype? What can we learn from him about how to share our convictions with others?*

- *When Paul shows enough familiarity with Greek and Roman writers to quote them spontaneously, is he "selling out" his own faith? How can openness to ideas and cultures other than our own allow us to move toward conversation rather than condemnation?*

Work together to create a list of practical ideas for being a positive, loving witness to non-Christians. Write your ideas on a board or chart.

WRAPPING UP

Notable Quote

According to [the Christian Inclusivist] view, it is possible for God to give the gift of salvation to those who have sought to love and serve God even if they have never heard the gospel or have not fully understood or accepted it. Inclusivists acknowledge that there are many people who have faith in God and a desire for salvation, but who may not fully understand where salvation comes from or the name by which salvation is given. They believe that in such cases, God looks at the heart and judges according to the light of the knowledge those persons have access to.

Inclusivism reminds us that the Christian gospel, the good news, is that we are saved by grace. In the New Testament, grace refers to God's kindness, love, care, work on our behalf, blessings, gifts, goodness, and salvation. But it is more than that—it is *undeserved*. God's grace is pure gift.

—Adam Hamilton

Closing Prayer

Dear God, we gather regularly to wrestle with questions about ourselves, about life's purpose, and about your call to service. We're thankful we can learn some of your truth. Please keep us from the hurtful arrogance that says we've figured it all out and have the right to condemn and condescend to others, either within our group or outside of it. Teach our hearts the ultimate truth—that you are love. Amen.

WEEK 4

WHEN BAD THINGS HAPPEN

Main Idea: If we want to get it right when it comes to how we speak and act in times of suffering, we need to carefully consider what we believe about how God works in the world and seek to be the hands, feet, and voice of Jesus to those who are suffering.

GETTING STARTED

Session Goals

This session is intended to help participants . . .
- question the assumptions they may have been taught regarding God's involvement in the affairs of the world, and consider that some of these assumptions not only may be wrong but also may serve to push people away from God
- explore a line of reasoning that helps to reconcile a loving God with a world filled with pain and suffering
- consider what insights the Book of Job offers regarding the problem of suffering
- stand with those who are suffering, offering the love and hope of Christ

Welcome / Important Reminders

Welcome participants and review the important reminders on p. 8.

Opening Prayer

Lord, life can be so hard at times. Suffering is part of the human experience because we live in a fallen, imperfect world. Like everyone who has come before us, we struggle to make sense of it all; and sometimes in our effort to make sense of it, we wind up saying and doing things that hurt others. Help us to sort through our questions, to question our assumptions, and to examine our beliefs carefully. Remind us that we do not have all the answers and never will, and that the most important question is not "Why?" but "What now?" We are comforted by the fact that you are familiar with our pain, that you are present with us through it, and that you promise to bring good from it. Teach us to share the comfort we have received from you with others, reaching out with compassion to be your hands, feet, and voice in a hurting world. Amen.

Biblical Foundation

> *Then Job replied:*
> *"I have heard many things like these;*
>   *miserable comforters are you all!*
> *Will your long-winded speeches never end?*
>   *What ails you that you keep on arguing?*
> *I also could speak like you,*
>   *if you were in my place;*
> *I could make fine speeches against you*
>   *and shake my head at you.*
> *But my mouth would encourage you;*
>   *comfort from my lips would bring you relief."*
>   *(Job 16:1-5, NIV)*

Opening Activity

Instruct participants to recall a difficult or painful time in their lives—a time when others knew of their pain and reached out with expressions of comfort. Invite participants to share some of the helpful and hurtful expressions of comfort they received—both words and deeds—and write these on a board or chart in two separate columns. (Caution participants not to use names or to share experiences or details involving anyone in the group.)

LEARNING TOGETHER

Video Presentation
Play the DVD segment for Week 4, *When Bad Things Happen.* Running Time: 19:48

Key Insights
1. When we say that everything happens for a reason, we're saying that bad things—even tragic or evil things—happen because God intends for them to happen. The challenge that comes with this line of thinking is this: How can we trust, love, and desire to serve a God who wills or causes bad things to happen?
2. Some of the long and commonly held assumptions about God's involvement in the affairs of our world—the things Christians sometimes say in the face of suffering and even blessing—not only may be wrong, but also may serve to push people away from God.
3. God's involvement in the world and in our lives is called providence. What we believe about providence determines how we respond when bad things happen.
4. Nearly all Christians agree that God is sovereign—the highest authority or supreme ruler—yet some also claim that God is actually controlling every dimension of the creation. This belief is sometimes referred to as the marionette view of divine providence. The Bible seems to teach the opposite of this view.
5. Whatever we say about God or attribute to God must line up with God's character as revealed in the Scriptures. The character of God revealed throughout the Scriptures is that of a kind, loving, and merciful Father—not a monster.

6. Much of what we blame God for is the result of humanity's sin and the realities of an imperfect world—such as sickness, disease, natural disasters, accidents, violence, and death. God accepts these realities, but God does not initiate them.

7. Typically God does not answer our prayers by intervening supernaturally, yet God can and sometimes does intervene in miraculous ways.

8. God does not cause bad things to happen, but when they do happen, God uses them to work for our good. God uses the difficult and tragic experiences of our lives to grow us and make us more like Christ.

9. When it comes to the problem of suffering, we must allow room for mystery, knowing that there is much we do not know and cannot understand.

10. The Book of Job is meant to challenge the assumption that you get what you deserve in life. It illustrates that we do not always have all the answers, and often our misguided responses bring pain rather than comfort to those who are suffering.

11. The church, the body of Christ, should be made up of people filled with compassion who carry one another through the difficult times. We are to be the hands, feet, and voice of Christ to those who are hurting.

12. Knowing that God loves us and that nothing can separate us from God's love (Romans 8:35-39) sustains us through the dark and difficult times.

Leader Extra

New Testament Insights on Suffering

Matthew 14:13-21

This story is typical of many. When Jesus met people with problems (whether illness, hunger, or any of the many other challenges humans face), he did not offer them a lecture about what they'd done wrong, or tell them God was teaching them a lesson. Instead, he had compassion and sought to make things better.

Luke 13:1-17

In Jesus' day, as in ours, many people were inclined to view tragedy and suffering as a divine punishment and/or object lesson. Jesus said they "got it wrong." He recognized the randomness of some tragedies and the role of evil in creating others. He was not interested in assigning blame but in bringing healing.

John 9:1-41

Jesus' disciples began this story convinced that the man they saw begging was born blind due either to his own or his parents' sins. When the story ended, the Pharisees were still sure of that (verse 34). Again, Jesus disagreed. God, he said, can bring good even out of tragedy, but that does not mean God caused it.

Romans 8:18-28, 35-39

Christians have sometimes applied this passage, especially verse 28, in hurtful ways. Note that verse 28 does NOT say God causes all things, nor that everything that happens is good. Instead, Paul affirms his triumphant faith that if we put our lives in God's hands, God will work for good IN all things.

2 Corinthians 4:5-18

The apostle Paul's language soars as he expresses his unshakable trust in the goodness of God's purposes. What matters most, he says, is not what's happening outside of us. We look to the unseen, and we know that God is always at work, renewing us inwardly no matter what circumstances we face.

1 Peter 5:6-10

Early Christian believers often faced persecution from the Roman government, alienation from their families, and economic hardship. Peter was convinced that God did not cause these hardships, and that God was still present and working for good even when believers suffered.

Leader Extra

Excerpt From *The Will of God*, by Leslie Weatherhead

The phrase "the will of God" is used so loosely, and the consequence of that looseness to our peace of mind is so serious, that I want to spend some time in thinking through with you the whole subject. . . . I sometimes think, there is nothing about which men and women are more confused.

Let me illustrate the confusion. I have a good friend whose dearly loved wife recently died. When she was dead, he said, "Well, I must just accept it. It is the will of God." But he is himself a doctor, and for weeks he had been fighting for her life. He had called in the best specialists in London. He had used all the devices of modern science, all the inventive apparatus by which the energies of nature can be used to fight disease. Was he all that time fighting *against* the will of God? If she had recovered, would he not have called her recovery the will of God? Yet surely we cannot have it both ways. The woman's recovery and the woman's death cannot equally be the will of God in the sense of being his intention. . . .

Here is a mother wringing her hands and weeping in anguish because her baby is dead. Her minister stands by her, longing to comfort her; but though his presence and prayers may offer consolation, he knows only too well that when the storm is raging it is too late to talk about the anchor that should have been put down before the storm began. What I mean is that it is so important that we should try to think clearly before disaster falls upon us. If we do, then in spite of all our grief we have a philosophy of life that steadies us as an anchor steadies a ship. If we do not, the storm is so furious that little can be done until it has abated. If only the minister could have injected into the mind of the woman his own belief about God! But that, alas! is impossible. In her anguish, this is what the woman said: "I suppose it is the will of God, *but if only the doctor had come in time he could have saved my baby.*" You see the confusion of thought. If the doctor had come in time, would he have been able to outwit the will of God?

—Leslie D. Weatherhead, *The Will of God*
(Abingdon, 1972); pp. 9–11. Used by permission.

For Further Study

Rebecca Laird's *The Will of God: A Workbook* (Abingdon, 1995) is an excellent small-group study based on Leslie Weatherhead's classic book *The Will of God.*

Group Discussion

Note: More questions are provided than you may have time for. Select those you would like your group to discuss.

1. Many Christians have the theological assumption that everything happens for a reason, or that everything that happens is God's will. Why do you think that this belief is so common? What are the challenges to this line of thinking?

2. How can an undeveloped or unexamined theology of evil and suffering cause us to say things that are hurtful rather than helpful to those who are suffering? (Skip the following question if you did the Opening Activity.) Have you ever been hurt by the comments of someone who was trying to offer comfort? Share as you are comfortable (without using names or sharing experiences or details involving anyone in the group).

3. Read aloud Leader Extra: "Excerpt From *The Will of God*, by Leslie Weatherhead." How are our thoughts about who God is and how God works in the world an "anchor" that steadies us when the storms of life come? Why is it essential for us to have this anchor securely in place prior to the coming of the storms? What can help us to do this?

4. What does it mean to say that God is "sovereign"? Do you believe it is possible for God to be sovereign yet not in

control of every dimension of the creation? Why or why not? What does the Bible say about God's sovereignty? How does your view of God's sovereignty affect your view of the way God works in a world of pain and suffering?

5. What do the stories in the Bible seem to teach about divine providence? How is free will—our ability to make choices—an argument against the marionette view of divine providence?

6. (Skip this question if you plan to do the Group Activity.) Read Luke 13:1-17. What can we learn from this exchange? If collapsing towers and killings by foreign soldiers are not "acts of God," what does cause them? What do you think Jesus would tell a grieving relative of someone killed in these tragedies?

7. What is the best "measuring stick" for the comments we make about God and the things we attribute to God? What do the Scriptures reveal about the character of God?

8. Much of what we blame God for is the result of humanity's sin and the realities of an imperfect world, such as sickness, violence, and natural disasters. Why do you think God allows us to experience the effects and consequences of these things?

9. Read Matthew 7:9-11 and Hebrews 12:4-11. According to these verses, how is God like a loving Parent? What would you say to someone who asks if trials and tragedies are God's way of disciplining us?

10. What is the distinction between the following two statements, and why is it significant? *God causes painful experiences or tragedies in order to teach us a lesson. God uses the difficult and tragic experiences of our lives to grow us and make us more like Christ.*

11. Read Romans 8:28. How does God "use" the difficult and tragic experiences of our lives? Share a time when God brought good through a painful experience in your life.

12. Would you agree that God chooses to work in the world in certain ways and does not ordinarily intervene supernaturally? Why or why not? Has God ever intervened in your life or the life of someone you know in a miraculous way? Share as you are comfortable.

13. When it comes to divine providence and the problem of suffering, why is it important to allow plenty of room for mystery? What kind of comforters are those who insist on a "black and white" theology of divine providence?

14. What assumption does the Book of Job challenge? Though it does not offer answers regarding the "why" of suffering, what does it teach us?

15. What does the apostle Paul's analogy of the church as the body of Christ tell us about our role in the lives of those who are suffering? How would you explain or describe what it means to show compassion for someone?

16. Read Romans 8:35-39. How can these verses help to sustain us through the dark and difficult times? Why is holding onto hope crucial in times of difficulty and tragedy?

17. How has this discussion helped or challenged you?

Group Activity

In advance of the group session, write each Scripture reference and corresponding commentary found in Leader Extra: "New Testament Insights on Suffering" on a separate index card. Divide participants into six groups and give each group an index card. Instruct the groups to read the Scripture passages aloud and discuss the commentary, noting any additional insights they have. Come back together and have one person from each group summarize their passage and the group's thoughts about it.

OR

Read aloud 2 Corinthians 4:5-18. Invite participants to respond to the following questions: When did you last feel hard-pressed, perplexed, or struck down? What habits or practices have you found helpful in accessing the spiritual strength God offers you so that you can keep gaining inner resilience and not be crushed by the challenges that come to you?

WRAPPING UP

Notable Quote

[This] is what the church looks like at its best—people filled with compassion who carry one another through the difficult times. . . . When bad things happen, the right response is to carefully consider how God works in the world, let go of our anger, and embrace God's love. It is as simple as saying, "I need you, God, and I trust you." Then, in time, God is able to use us to minister to others who are hurting, bringing them compassion, comfort, courage, and hope in their time of need. This is the right response when bad things happen. And when we get it right, others are drawn to the love and hope of God through us.

—Adam Hamilton

Closing Prayer

Dear God, we gather regularly to wrestle with questions about ourselves, about life's purpose, and about your call to service. We're thankful we can learn some of your truth. Please keep us from the hurtful arrogance that says we've figured it all out and have the right to condemn and condescend to others, either within our group or outside of it. Teach our hearts the ultimate truth—that you are love. Amen.

WEEK 5

IN DEALING WITH HOMOSEXUALITY

Main Idea: We get it wrong when we speak and act in ways that bring harm and alienation to God's homosexual children; but we get it right when, despite our questions and uncertainty, we express the love and welcome of Jesus Christ.

GETTING STARTED

Session Goals

This session is intended to help participants . . .

- acknowledge that most young adults believe Christians are anti-homosexual—unloving in the ways they interact with, talk to, and talk about homosexuals—and this is one of the primary reasons young adults are turning away from the church
- recognize that young adults often see the issue of homosexuality very differently than those who have come before them
- consider that the underlying issue is the nature of Scripture and its authority for our lives
- understand the idea of progressive revelation, which says that the promptings of God's Spirit were understood in the light of the concepts, ideas, and presuppositions of the times in which the biblical authors lived
- note that Wesley's quadrilateral can help us to rightly handle the Scriptures

- consider the possibility that God's perspective on homosexuality may be different than what is in Leviticus or in Paul's letter to the church at Rome
- recognize that Jesus put people before rules
- understand that although Christians are divided on the issue of homosexuality, we all can agree to demonstrate the warmth, welcome, and love of Jesus Christ to men and women who are gay and lesbian

Welcome / Important Reminders

Welcome participants and review the important reminders on p. 8.

Opening Prayer

Dear God, we confess that we have not treated all of your children with kindness, respect, and love. If we had, so many young adults would not have said that we Christians show special contempt toward homosexual individuals. They have observed that, generally speaking, we have not shown the love of Jesus to our brothers and sisters who are gay and lesbian. We have not followed your basic command to love our neighbors as ourselves. Forgive us, Lord. Open our hearts and minds and fill us with your Holy Spirit so that we may discuss differing ideas and perspectives without debating or arguing or dividing. Despite our questions and our uncertainty about this issue, our desire is to glorify you by demonstrating the love of Jesus to all people. Amen.

Biblical Foundation

Then [Peter] heard a voice saying, "Get up, Peter; kill and eat." But [he] said, "By no means, Lord; for I have never eaten anything that is profane or unclean." The voice said to him again, a second time, "What God has made clean, you must not call profane." And as [Peter] talked with [Cornelius], he went in and found that many had assembled; and he said to them, "You yourselves know that it is unlawful for a Jew to associate with or to visit a Gentile;

but God has shown me that I should not call anyone profane or unclean." (Acts 10:13-15, 27-28)

The Samaritan woman said to him, "You are a Jew
and I am a Samaritan woman. How can you ask me for a
drink?" (For Jews do not associate with Samaritans.) Jesus
answered her, "If you knew the gift of God and who it is
that asks you for a drink, you would have asked him and he
would have given you living water." "Sir," the woman
said, "you have nothing to draw with and the well is deep.
Where can you get this living water? Are you greater than
our father Jacob, who gave us the well and drank from it
himself, as did also his sons and his flocks and herds?" Jesus
answered, "Everyone who drinks this water will be thirsty
again, but whoever drinks the water I give him will never
thirst. Indeed, the water I give him will become in him a
spring of water welling up to eternal life." The woman said
to him, "Sir, give me this water so that I won't get thirsty
and have to keep coming here to draw water." He told her,
"Go, call your husband and come back." "I have no husband," she replied. Jesus said to her, "You are right when
you say you have no husband. The fact is, you have had
five husbands, and the man you now have is not your husband. What you have just said is quite true." . . . Then,
leaving her water jar, the woman went back to the town
and said to the people, "Come, see a man who told me
everything I ever did. Could this be the Christ?" They
came out of the town and made their way toward him.
(John 4:9-18, 28-30, NIV)

Opening Activity

Read aloud the following: *Tony and Peggy Campolo are deeply
committed to Christ and to each other. They disagree on homosexuality, but they agree, eloquently and powerfully, about how Christians
should treat all people, including homosexuals. In this brief excerpt from
a talk they gave in 1996, Tony explains that it is possible for individuals to differ over a critical issue without division or alienation:*

I have to announce that we are two people who. . . . have very, very divergent views. . . . I for instance believe that the Bible does not allow for same gender sexual marriage. I do not believe that same gender sexual intercourse is permissible if you read the Bible as I do. Peggy believes in monogamous relationships. . . . She would hold to a belief that within the framework of evangelical Christianity, gay marriages are permissible. . . . We're saying . . . that it is possible for two people to differ intensely over a crucial issue and not get a divorce. . . . This above all should be communicated, that it is necessary for us to respect each other across our differences, love each other and recognize we belong together even if we don't agree. . . . Let not an issue destroy the fellowship. Let not a difference of opinion alienate us.

—Tony Campolo speaking at North Park College Chapel
(www.bridges-across.org/ba/campolo.htm)

Discuss:

- *Do you agree that it is possible for deeply committed Christians—whether they be relatives, neighbors, fellow church members, or even complete strangers—to disagree on the issue of homosexuality in a respectful, peaceable way that encourages fellowship rather than alienation?*
- *What can help us to do this?*

LEARNING TOGETHER

Video Presentation

Play the DVD segment for Week 5, *In Dealing With Homosexuality*.

Running Time: 19:47

Key Insights

1. Young adults who are outside the church are criticizing those of us who are inside the church for not being more

like Jesus in how we interact with, talk to, and talk about homosexuals. Our treatment of homosexuals has become one of the primary reasons young adults are turning away from the church.

2. Young adults see the issue of homosexuality very differently from those who came before them.

3. Homosexuality is the most divisive issue in the church today, and it is important to recognize how serious of an issue this is for both sides in the divide.

4. When it comes to the debate over homosexuality within the Christian faith, the underlying issue is the nature of Scripture and its authority for our lives.

5. The Bible is more complicated than a simple, literal interpretation allows. John Wesley, the founder of Methodism, believed that Christians draw on four sources as they seek to discern God's will in their lives, and the lives of their communities. These four sources or guides came to be known after Wesley's time as the Wesleyan quadrilateral:

   - Scripture – the primary basis for our faith and practice
   - Tradition – the church's theological, ethical, and biblical reflections over the last 2,000 years, which includes the work of scholars, commentators, ethicists, and theologians
   - Reason – our rational minds and scientific knowledge
   - Experience – our own life experience and the witness of the Spirit

6. "Progressive revelation" is the idea that the promptings of God's Spirit were understood in the light of the concepts, ideas, and presuppositions of the times in which the biblical authors lived. The authors were speaking to the people of their times, addressing the issues, needs, and challenges of their time. Progressive revelation does not give us the freedom to find a rationalization for setting aside every Scripture we do not like. Rather, it prompts us to engage in serious study and reflection when we are faced with serious

issues, rather than simply quoting a verse or two and considering the matter settled.

7. Unlike any other words about God in the Scripture, Jesus is the pure and complete Word of God. Thus, we read all Scripture in the light of what Jesus said and did.

8. Progressive revelation leads us to be open to the possibility that God's perspective on homosexuality may be different than what is in Leviticus or in Paul's letter to the church at Rome. It may be that heterosexuality is God's ideal and intention for humanity; our bodies themselves bear witness to this, as does the Bible's teaching about God creating us male and female. But God's compassion and understanding toward persons who do not fit these norms—whose fundamental wiring seems to be oriented towards same-sex attraction—are undoubtedly greater than the Scriptures would indicate.

9. Jesus did not lecture the woman at the well on the evils of divorce or cohabitation but simply offered her grace. Jesus knew that people come before rules.

10. Although we Christians are divided on the issue of homosexuality, we all can agree to offer men and women who are gay and lesbian the warmth and welcome and love of Jesus Christ—as individuals and as the church.

Leader Extra

Two Opposing Views on Homosexuality

Homosexuality Is Not Incompatible With Christian Teaching

Some Christians see homosexuality not as a willful decision to act in sinful, immoral, or perverted ways, but as a natural way that a small percentage of the population is either biologically or psychological "wired." They do not see how two people of the same sex loving one another deeply in a committed relationship is offensive, immoral, or sinful.

Christians who defend homosexuality feel called to embrace the outcasts of our day as Jesus embraced those of his day. Their reasons for this position include the following:

- *Homosexuality is not a choice.* Sexual orientation is determined from the womb, though some homosexuality may be shaped by early childhood experiences.
- *Homosexuality in teens often leads to despair.* If the church were more open to homosexuals, we would be better able to help young people who are homosexuals feel loved and accepted—by other Christians and by God.
- *Jesus wouldn't reject homosexuals but would welcome them.* Jesus never once said anything about homosexuality. In contrast to Jesus' compassionate approach, there are Christians who have implicitly and explicitly pushed homosexuals out of the church and away from God.
- *Some homosexuals have the gifts, calling, and faith to be in ministry.* There are those who are deeply committed to Christ and have a profound sense of calling to ministry, but who wrestle with homosexuality. Surely God intends such persons to use their God-given gifts for ministry.
- *The biblical texts that refer to homosexuality have not always been interpreted with sensitivity and in light of new cultural and scientific understandings.* (See Leader Extra: "The Bible and Homosexuality.")

Homosexuality Is Incompatible With Christian Teaching

Other Christians see homosexuality as incompatible with Christian teaching. Their reasons for this position include the following:

- *The witness of the Bible is explicit.* The clear teaching of both the Old and New Testaments is that homosexual intimacy is not God's plan for what we do with our bodies, just as some acts of heterosexual intimacy are also not part of God's plan. (See the following Leader Extra: "The Bible and Homosexuality.")

- *God prohibits certain things because God loves us and knows these things bring harm.* Homosexual relationships often bring harm to those involved, both emotionally and physically.
- *All are born broken; we all struggle with our human condition.* Some people are born with a predisposition toward homosexuality, but this by itself does not indicate that God has made one to be, or wishes one to be, homosexual. We all are born with an orientation to sin. By nature and from birth we struggle with our longing for power and wealth, our tendency to be self-centered and self-absorbed, and with a host of issues related to misuse of our sexuality, not simply homosexuality. Yet God encourages us to allow the Spirit to work in us to rise above these temptations.
- *God's help makes anything possible.* Some believe that homosexuals are able—with the help of counselors, friends, and the Holy Spirit—to see their desires reshaped and sexual energy redirected toward male-female relationships. They acknowledge that this transformation is not easy but is possible as evidenced by the testimonies of those who have made this change with God's help. Other homosexuals choose lifelong celibacy, a choice affirmed as among the highest callings by Jesus and the apostle Paul (Matthew 19:10-12; 1 Corinthians 7:8-9, 32-35). Both Jesus and Paul indicated that God's power is strong enough to help us either overcome our struggles or live with them in a way that honors God.

Leader Extra

The Bible and Homosexuality

New Views

(1) The biblical texts prohibiting homosexual behavior refer to certain types of homosexual behavior that are generally condemned as reprehensible—most often slavery,

prostitution, and pederasty—and not to monogamous homosexual practice.

(2) In biblical times, the concept of "orientation" was not understood; they did not know that some persons are born predisposed to homosexual feelings and drives.

(3) This is a different time period, and the prohibitions against homosexuality—like those against women speaking in the church—are tied to the cultural and historical setting and do not represent the timeless Word of God on the issue.

Traditional Views

(1) Leviticus 18:22 and 20:13 say that a man should not lie with another man. Some point out that these laws are included in the "holiness code" of Leviticus, which includes other prohibitions that we do not hold binding today, which is true. But their immediate context is a section dealing with sexual practices God does not wish for us to participate in.

(2) 1 Timothy 1:10 provides a list of categories of "sinners," which includes the Greek word *arsenokoitai*, which was usually translated as "homosexual." All of the practices in this list are said to be contrary to sound teaching and what conforms to the gospel.

(3) 1 Corinthians 6:9-11 enumerates those who are living lives contrary to God's plans, including male prostitutes and homosexual offenders. Some note that these two types of "offenders" could be linked together to refer to a specific vice called pederasty (a practice in which an adult male dominates a submissive minor male for sexual purposes). Others note that by condemning pederasty, the passage would be condemning what may have been the dominant and most culturally acceptable form of homosexual practice in Paul's day, though it is not acceptable today.

(4) In Romans 1, Paul includes homosexual practice as an expression of our sinful nature.

Some Christians suggest that Scriptures related to homosexuality are culturally bound, such as Scriptures related to women's rights or slavery, and are not relevant today. This idea is explored in chapter 5 of the participant book. Other Christians believe that the opposite is true. Consider the following argument.

In the case of slavery, this practice was a dominant cultural, political, and economic factor of life in biblical times, and the biblical authors could not conceive of a world without slavery. Hence, they gave guidelines for how slaves should live and how masters should treat their slaves. In the case of women's rights, the culture said that women were property, but Paul said they were to be loved as Christ loved the church. Nevertheless, Paul cautioned the churches not to arouse the suspicions of their neighbors by encouraging women to engage in what would be considered outrageous behavior for the time by teaching or speaking in church. Again, Paul was influenced by his culture rather than confronting the cultural norm. But in the case of homosexuality, Paul adopted a critical stance toward the surrounding culture, which generally accepted homosexual practice. Despite approval from the culture, Paul said that homosexuality was not God's will.

Leader Extra
Mercy Over Judgment in the New Testament

Matthew 9:9-13
In Jesus' day, as in ours, many religious people were sure that holiness meant not only avoiding "sin" and "sinners," but also showing your virtue by loudly condemning such "unworthy" people. Jesus never associated himself with that view. In fact, he often went out of his way to challenge that attitude.

Luke 7:36-39
Jesus' "righteous" host is shocked that Jesus doesn't condemn this woman. Jesus is more dismayed by his host's self-righteous arrogance than by the woman's checkered past. It's clear he knows

her troubled history, but more than that, he knows her. It is often difficult for us to see the real human being behind actions that make us uneasy. Jesus calls us to show mercy and love to those who are socially or religiously ostracized. Realizing that we have been forgiven much increases our gratitude to God and changes the way we treat others.

John 8:2-11

John says this was a set-up (verse 6), which it clearly was. Where was the woman's partner? (It's impossible to commit adultery alone!) But worse, this was life-and-death. The accusers were clamoring to stone the woman to death. Jesus' mercy and compassion were, literally, lifesaving. Jesus said, in effect, "In order to condemn others, you'd need these credentials: anyone who is sinless gets to cast the first stone." None of us qualifies to be a stone-thrower. (Jesus would have qualified—but since he was sinless, he wasn't interested in throwing stones!) This story should move our lives in the direction of greater freedom, peace, and joy.

James 2:8-13

James found the same unforgiving spirit that had hounded Jesus showing up in early Christian churches. In words that evoke Jesus' teaching in Matthew 7, he says that we need to watch our attitude toward others, because in the end, mercy triumphs over judgment in God's world. James refers to the command to love your neighbor as yourself as a "royal law." Relating to others with mercy rather than condemnation brings about greater freedom for them and for us.

For Further Study

The website for Bridges Across the Divide (http://www. bridges-across.org/ba/christiandebate.htm) provides links to numerous articles debating both sides of the homosexuality issue from a Christian perspective, including the full transcript of the talk "Is the Homosexual My Neighbor?" by Tony and Peggy Campolo, excerpted in the Opening Activity.

Group Discussion

Note: More questions are provided than you may have time for. Select those you would like your group to discuss.

1. Does it surprise you to know that the majority of young adults outside the church view Christians as anti-homosexual? Why or why not? Why do you think this criticism has become one of the primary reasons young adults are turning away from the church?

2. Why do you think young adults see the issue of homosexuality so differently from the generations that came before them?

3. Why do you think homosexuality is the most divisive issue in the church today, and why is it such a serious issue for both sides in the divide? What is at stake?

4. Review and discuss Leader Extra: "Two Opposing Views on Homosexuality." Which points or arguments do you find compelling?

5. When it comes to the debate over homosexuality within the Christian faith, what has been suggested to be the underlying issue, and why? Do you agree that the debate essentially comes down to this issue? Why or why not?

6. Do you agree with the idea that the Bible is more complicated than a simple, literal interpretation allows? Why or why not? How can the Wesleyan quadrilateral (Scripture, tradition, reason, experience) help us to rightly interpret Scripture?

7. What is "progressive revelation"? Explain the concept in your own words.

8. Critics say that the idea of progressive revelation gives us permission to pick and choose which verses in the Bible are no longer applicable to us. Supporters say that it prompts us to engage in serious study and reflection when we are faced with serious issues, rather than to simply quote a verse or two and consider the matter settled. What are your thoughts about the benefits and/or pitfalls of progressive revelation?

9. How is the idea of progressive revelation relevant to the homosexuality debate within the Christian faith? (See pp. 86–90 in the participant book and Leader Extra: "The Bible and Homosexuality.") Are you willing to be *open to the possibility* that God's perspective on homosexuality may be different than what was captured in Leviticus or by Paul? Why or why not?

10. Regardless of what you believe about progressive revelation or the issue of homosexuality, how do you think God wants us to treat men and women who are homosexual? How did Jesus treat those who were looked down upon or condemned by society?

11. Read aloud John 4:9-18, 29-30. Why do you think Jesus did not lecture the woman at the well on the evils of divorce or cohabitation but simply offered her grace? How else does this story illustrate that Jesus put people before rules?

12. Read aloud Luke 7:36-39. Why is Jesus' "righteous" host shocked? Jesus is more dismayed by his host's self-righteous arrogance than by the woman's checkered past. It's clear he knows her troubled history, but more than that, he knows her. Why do you think it is often difficult for us to see the real human being behind actions that make us uneasy? When, if ever, have you shown love to someone who was socially or religiously ostracized? Share as you are comfortable. (See Leader Extra: "Mercy Over Judgment in the New Testament" for additional Scriptures to explore.)

13. Read aloud John 8:2-11. Imagine yourself huddled on the ground in the place where the woman in this story was, and then picture Jesus saying to you, "I don't condemn you." How were Jesus' mercy and compassion literally life-saving? How can that message move our lives in the direction of greater freedom, peace, and joy? Now imagine you are one of the crowd, holding a stone in your hand. Jesus said, in effect, "In order to condemn others and cast stones, you must be sinless." Do any of us qualify to be a

stone-thrower? (See Leader Extra: "Mercy Over Judgment in the New Testament" for additional Scriptures to explore.)

14. Although we Christians are divided on the issue of homosexuality, why is it so important that we agree to offer men and women who are homosexual the warmth, welcome, and love of Jesus Christ? How can we do this as individuals? As the church?

15. How has this discussion helped or challenged you?

Group Activity

Remind participants of the Opening Activity and invite them to listen as you continue reading from the talk given by Tony and Peggy Campolo in 1996. (Note: Provide the website address found below and encourage participants to read the full transcript, which presents in detail Tony's and Peggy's differing views regarding what the Bible says about homosexuality, on their own.)

> *Tony:* I don't know what else we're about, but we [Christians] are not to be about creating hatred toward the [homosexuals] of this world, whatever our views are. And I am a conservative on this issue. I believe that same gender sexual intercourse . . . [is] not what is at issue here. . . . What's at trial here is the church of Jesus Christ. . . . Take your stand and be bold for Christ and say this, that whether we agree or do not agree on this issue, we will not allow discrimination and hatred and meanness to be directed at people who did not choose their identity, number one, and cannot choose to get out of an orientation as simply as those evangelists who preach so blithely suggest. . . . It's important for somebody who preaches that people have to be born again according to the Bible to stand up and say [that] being born again means . . . you love people.

Tell participants that Peggy closed the talk by posing several questions. Invite participants to respond to these questions, which have been modified for group discussion:

- What kind of a Jesus do gay and lesbian people see in you? In your church?
- Do homosexual people see and hear you/your church as a friend? Is your church a safe, welcoming place, or do they view your church as a danger zone—perhaps the danger zone they're afraid to risk passing through even though they might like to look more closely at your God? If your honest answer is the latter, what can you do to make your church a safe, welcoming place?
- Jesus said that the world will know we are Christians by our love. What can we do to show the world that we are Christians who love all people, including men and women who are homosexual?

(Tony and Peggy Campolo, speaking at North Park College Chapel. See www.bridges-across.org/ba/campolo.htm for a complete transcript.)

WRAPPING UP

Notable Quote

[My] understanding of the nature of Scripture opened the door for me to see this issue differently than I once had but when I began to know and care about people who are homosexual, my heart truly changed. . . . I think of Mary. I have been her pastor since she was two. . . . Mary recently told me she was homosexual. I cried as I read some of the things other Christians have said to her. I think of Aaron, who grew up in our youth group, served on our church council, and who was quite serious about wanting to follow Jesus Christ. I think of Kristin, who I watched grow up. She is now a schoolteacher and in a covenant relationship with her partner. Many of my questions about homosexuality are yet to be answered. . . . But this one thing I am certain of—I don't want be a church that turns away young adults like Mary, Aaron, or Kristin.   —Adam Hamilton

Closing Prayer

Dear God, we experience a rush of power and pleasure when we feel superior to others. Keep us mindful of how much it hurts when someone else looks down on us. Help us learn from Jesus, who—though he was sinless (more precisely, because he was sinless)—is the most merciful person who ever lived. Make us more like him. Amen.

WEEK 6

WHEN CHRISTIANS GET IT RIGHT

Main Idea: When we Christians get it right, we love as Jesus loved, and that is a powerful witness that has the capacity to change the world.

GETTING STARTED

Session Goals

This session is intended to help participants . . .

- recognize that the gospel is all about love and the goal of the Christian life is to love as Jesus loved
- understand the kind of love that Christians are to show
- consider the two great commandments of Jesus
- realize that if they are growing as Christians, they will be ever deepening their love for God and ever growing in their love for others
- explore love as the central Christian ethic
- recognize that sacrificial love involves taking risks, being inconvenienced, and loving those who are unworthy

Welcome / Important Reminders

Welcome participants and review the important reminders on p. 8.

Opening Prayer

Dear God, we confess that we have a tendency to get it wrong. It's called sin, and it affects every single one of us. Thankfully, you sent your Son, Jesus, not for the sake of perfect people—because there are none of those—but for those who are prone to get it wrong, offering us grace. We praise you for your love, mercy, and forgiveness. Still, we acknowledge that the Christian life does not stop at forgiveness. You call us to be holy—to be sanctified or set apart—and holiness looks like love. Jesus said that the world would know we are Christians by our love. Help us to love as Jesus loved and, as a result, to draw others to him. Amen.

Biblical Foundation

"Beloved, since God loved us so much, we also ought to love one another. No one has ever seen God; if we love one another, God lives in us, and his love is perfected in us. . . . So we have known and believe the love that God has for us. God is love, and those who abide in love abide in God, and God abides in them. . . . We love because he first loved us. Those who say, 'I love God,' and hate their brothers or sisters, are liars; for those who do not love a brother or sister whom they have seen, cannot love God whom they have not seen. The commandment we have from him is this: those who love God must love their brothers and sisters also." (1 John 4:11-12, 16, 19-21)

Opening Activity

Invite participants to call out words and phrases that describe Jesus' character as you write them on a board or chart. Continue this process until no one has anything else to contribute. Be sure that the word *love* or *loving* is included.

Discuss:

- *If we had to pick only one word or phrase that best describes Jesus, do you think "love" would be a good choice? Why?* (Circle the word *love/loving*.)

70

- *When we get it right as Christians, we love as Jesus loved. What might it "look like" for us to love as Jesus loved?*

Invite participants to suggest practical, everyday ways we can love as Jesus loved. Add these ideas to the board/chart.

LEARNING TOGETHER

Video Presentation
Play the DVD segment for Week 6, *When Christians Get It Right*. Running Time: 18:48

Key Insights
1. The gospel in one word is *love*. Jesus commanded us to love God with our entire beings and our neighbors as ourselves. The goal of the Christian life is summed up by these two commandments. Jesus said that the world will know we are his disciples by our love (John 13:34-35).
2. These two great commands to love—to love God and to love neighbor—define Christian life. When we are unsure of what the right thing to do is, we simply need to ask ourselves this question: In this situation, what is the most loving thing I can do?
3. The kind of love Jesus was referring to was not a feeling but a way of looking at, thinking about, and acting toward others that involves seeking their best, putting their needs before your own, and practicing kindness toward them at some personal cost—even when that kindness is undeserved.
4. The parable of the good Samaritan shows us how to love as Jesus loved: sacrificially. This kind of love is willing to be inconvenienced, to take risks, and to do what is right and kind and caring even to those who don't deserve it.

5. Every human being is afflicted with the tendency to get it wrong; we call this sin. Christianity does not invite perfect people to join up. It invites people who are prone to get it wrong, and it offers them grace. It is about forgiveness, not perfection.

6. The Christian life, however, does not stop at forgiveness. The aim of the Christian life is to get it right. Theologians call this aim "sanctification"—being made holy—and holiness looks like love.

7. The proof of spiritual growth is found in the practice of love.

8. The most compelling argument for Christianity is a Christian who demonstrates the love of God selflessly to another. When we Christians get it right, we share the love of God we have experienced through Jesus Christ—a love that is sacrificial, unconditional, filled with mercy, and ultimately life transforming.

9. God's love compels us to want to be more loving. The Holy Spirit and the disciplines of the Christian life are all aimed at helping us to know and live God's love.

Leader Extra

New Testament Writings on Love
(with questions for reflection/discussion)

Matthew 5:13-16 (Salt and Light)

Here Jesus talks about how we are to be salt and light in the world, pointing others to God. We do this for God's glory, not our own. We are not being salt and light when our motivation for doing good deeds is to be seen and praised. On the other hand, when we do good unaffectedly, others are moved to praise God.

- What does it mean to be salt and light?
- What is the difference between doing good selfishly, from a wish to be seen and praised, and doing it unaffectedly, so that others are moved to praise God?

- How, if at all, has it become more natural over time for you to let your light shine?

Matthew 5:43-48 (Jesus Tells Us to Love Our Enemies)

Jesus says that God causes it to rain on the just and the unjust alike. We are not to limit our help and efforts to bless to only the people we like or consider "worthy." Rather, we are to bless anyone who needs it. It is not necessary to have mushy, affectionate feelings about those we are helping. We simply choose to act for their good despite what they may have done to us. Making these hard choices helps us to grow in character and maturity. John Wesley studied these verses and said we can become "perfect in love." This does not mean we never sin; it means that we have a deep heart desire to love God and all our human "neighbors." According to Jesus, that's getting it right.

- How often are you tempted to limit your help and your efforts to bless only the people you like or consider "worthy"?
- How can you become more like God in your willingness to bless anyone who needs it?
- How do you understand the idea of loving your enemies?
- What does it mean to become "perfect in love"?

Matthew 22:34-40 (The Two Great Commandments of Jesus)

Jesus says that everything the Bible teaches—all the truths we know about what God wants—"hang" or "depend" on these two commands. In other words, any other truth has value only as it leads us to more fully love God and all our neighbors. Loving God and loving neighbor are inextricably connected. We cannot love our neighbor if we do not love God. And the more we love God, the more we will want to love our neighbor.

- What do you believe makes these two commands so essential?
- Can you recall a time when a belief you held led you to be unloving, even without realizing it?

- How well do you think you can love your neighbor as yourself if you don't have healthy ways of loving and caring for yourself? How well have you learned to nurture and value yourself? (Note: If participants struggle with this, they might find Mindy Caliguire's book *Discovering Soul Care* helpful.)

Luke 15:11-24 (The Parable of the Prodigal Son)

Few characters in Jesus' teaching are less "deserving" than this grating, ungrateful son. Yet Jesus shows the father running to meet his son and welcoming him in lavish ways the son wouldn't have dared ask for. He's calling us to get it right, to love others (even the "undeserving") as lavishly as God does. Jesus told this story to answer a complaint from the religious leaders that he welcomed sinners—even ate with them (Luke 15:2).

- How is this parable an example of God's lavish love?
- How do you react to the idea of God—and God's family, your church—welcoming people you consider sinners? How, if at all, have your feelings changed over time?
- Have you ever identified with the prodigal son? How were you received by those you considered righteous?
- How does the joy of the father's welcome celebration speak to your heart about your heavenly Parent's welcome of you?

Romans 12:9-21 (The Apostle Paul Writes About Love)

Here the apostle Paul describes in considerable detail what "getting it right" with one another looks like. But we don't only get it right with our close friends. A deeper key, says Paul, is to let God teach us how to get it right even with those who consider themselves our enemies. Paul quotes Proverbs 25:21-22 as a divine guideline about how to treat "your enemy." "Heaping burning coals" on someone's head is showing them such kindness and love that they will realize how badly they have treated you.

- What historical or contemporary figures can you think of who practiced in visible, public ways the principle of overcoming evil with good? How can we apply that principle in the personal relationships we're involved in every day?
- How would you explain the image that says treating the enemy kindly is like "heaping burning coals" on his head? Have you ever tried this approach? What were the results in the relationship? In your inner life?

1 Corinthians 13:1-13 (The Love Chapter)

This is essentially a lyrical description of when Christians get it right. Note the things love doesn't do—the signs of getting it wrong. Even more, note the things that love does, because these are the qualities, both inward and outward, that God's Spirit will increasingly grow in our lives.

- Which of the items listed in verses 4-7 do you value most from someone else?
- Which is the most challenging for you to offer to another person?
- What are some ways you might open your life to God's influence so that you can grow in these qualities?

Group Discussion

Note: More questions are provided than you may have time for. Select those you would like your group to discuss.

1. How would you explain what it means to say that the gospel in one word is *love*?
2. Read aloud Matthew 22:34-40. Jesus says that everything the Bible teaches—all the truths we know about what God wants—"hang" or "depend" on these two commands. What does this mean? What makes these two commands so essential?
3. How does the first great commandment differ from the Shema? Why do you think Jesus made this word change?

4. What is the second great commandment, according to Jesus? Why do you think Jesus elevated this command from Leviticus 19:18 to this level?

5. Do you agree with John Wesley, the founder of Methodism, that "there is no holiness without social holiness"—in other words, you cannot pursue holiness if you are not engaged in loving your neighbor? Why or why not?

6. Read 1 John 4:20. What is the relationship between love for God and love for neighbor? Do you believe it is possible to do one without the other? Why or why not?

7. How do the two great commandments of Jesus define Christian ethics? How can looking at situations through the lens of love help us to make moral and ethical decisions?

8. What is the greatest example of love, and how did Jesus model this for us?

9. Read aloud Luke 10:29-37. How does this parable illustrate the commandment to love your neighbor as yourself? How was the Samaritan a neighbor to the injured man? In what ways was his demonstration of love sacrificial? (How was he inconvenienced, what risks did he take, and what did he give up?)

10. Which question do you tend to ask more often: "What will happen to me if I stop to help?" or "What will happen to this person if I don't stop to help?" Why does love always put the needs of the other before oneself? What can help us to do this?

11. If Christianity is about forgiveness, not perfection, why is it important for us to "get it right"—to strive for holiness? What do we call this process of being made holy? What is the proof or evidence of our sanctification—our spiritual growth?

12. Respond to the following statement: *The most compelling argument for Christianity is a Christian who demonstrates the love of God selflessly to another.* Read aloud Colossians 3:9-14.

How can applying these verses help us to be compelling witnesses for Christ and Christianity?

13. How has this discussion helped or challenged you?

Group Activity

In advance of the group session, write each of the Scripture references, corresponding commentary, and discussion questions found in Leader Extra: "New Testament Writings on Love" on a separate index card. Divide participants into six groups and give each group an index card. Instruct the groups to read the Scripture passages and commentary aloud and then discuss the questions. Come back together and have one person from each group briefly summarize the passage and their thoughts about it.

OR

Write the following two headings on a board or chart: "Signs of Getting It Wrong" and "Signs of Getting It Right." Have two participants stand at the board/chart, one beside each column, with markers in hand. Ask another participant to slowly read aloud 1 Corinthians 13:1-13. The volunteers at the board/chart are to listen for words and phrases that fit their respective columns and list them accordingly.

Read through the passage a second time and invite participants to help identify or reword any ideas that were not listed.

Discuss: *How can these lists help us to love as Jesus loved?*

WRAPPING UP

Notable Quote

When we are unsure of what the right thing to do is, we simply need to ask ourselves this question: In this situation, what is the most loving thing I can do? . . . This question also helps to point us toward the kind of love Jesus was talking about. It is not some sappy, romantic, or feel-good kind of love. The kind of love he was referring to was not a feeling but a way of looking, thinking about, and acting toward others that involves seeking their best, putting their needs before your own, and practicing kindness toward them at some personal cost—even when that kindness is undeserved. Jesus himself defined what this love looks like on multiple occasions. He told us to love our enemies. Clearly this is not a feeling but a way of acting toward them that seeks their good even though they don't deserve it. He told us that the greatest example of this love is actually laying down one's life for another. He then lay down his own life for humankind through his suffering and death on the cross.

—Adam Hamilton

Closing Prayer

Gracious God, trying to "get it right" can feel so complicated—it sometimes seems there are so many "do's" and "don'ts." But Jesus boiled it down to loving you and loving our neighbors. We want to live that way. Guide us and teach us day by day as we become the people you are calling us to be. Amen.

Note to Leader: You may choose to view the bonus video, *Meet John* (Running Time: 6:34), in which John describes his struggle with the church, at the close of the final session.

CPSIA information can be obtained at www.ICGtesting.com
Printed in the USA
LVOW01s1728010814

397123LV00003B/3/P